For Caryl, without whose support and
encouragement from the very beginning
none of this would have been possible.

B.R.

Tilbury House Publishers
12 Starr Street, Thomaston, Maine 04861
www.tilburyhouse.com

First US edition 2021
ISBN: 978-0-88448-916-0

Original English language edition first published by Ladybird Books Ltd
20 Vauxhall Bridge Road, London, SW1V 2SA, UK
Copyright © Ben Rothery, 2019
The moral right of the author/illustrator has been asserted. All rights reserved.

Printed in China
A CIP catalog record for this book is available from the British Library
ISBN: 978-0-241-43553-3

Measurements

You'll see a few metric measurements in this book. Metric measurements are used in most of the world, but a few countries (including the US) still use the Imperial system of inches, feet, ounces, and pounds. Here are some conversion formulas to get from one system to the other.

Length

To convert meters to feet, multiply by 3.281. To convert centimeters to inches, divide by 2.54.

- 1 meter (or metre) = 39.37 inches, or about 3 feet; 1 foot = 0.305 meter; 1 yard = 0.914 meter.
- 1 centimeter (or centimetre) = 0.39 inch, less than half an inch; 1 inch = 2.54 centimeters.
- 1 millimeter = 0.039 inch; 1 inch = 25.4 millimeters.
- 1 kilometer = 0.62 mile; 1 mile = 1.609 kilometers.

Weight/Mass

To convert grams to ounces, divide by 28.35. To convert kilograms to pounds, multiply by 2.205.

- 1 gram = 0.035 ounce; 1 ounce = 28.35 grams.
- 1 kilogram = 2.205 pounds; 1 pound = 0.454 kilogram; 1 ton = 2,000 pounds or 907 kilograms; 1 metric ton = 1,000 kilograms.

Ocean Planet

Animals of the Sea and Shore

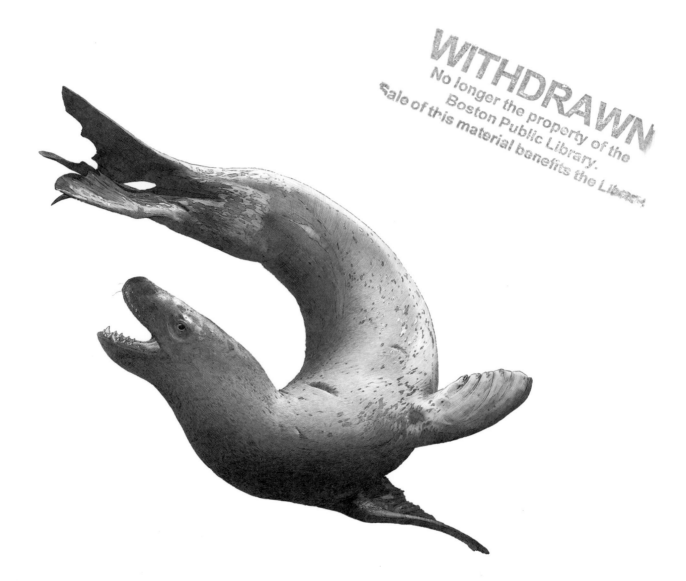

BEN ROTHERY

TILBURY HOUSE PUBLISHERS, THOMASTON, MAINE

Contents

Striped marlin
Kajikia audax

INTRODUCTION

Life on Earth is shaped by water, and only survives here because of it. Our five great oceans – the Atlantic, the Pacific, the Indian, the Arctic and the Antarctic (Southern) – cover more than 70 per cent of the Earth's surface and hold 97 per cent of its water. We might imagine the oceans to be separate from one another but, in reality, there is just one immense planet-spanning ocean. This vast blue wilderness contains somewhere between half and three quarters of all life on Earth, including the biggest and most numerous creatures ever to live. The oceans also contain our planet's tallest mountain and mountain range, and the deepest trench. It is from the oceans that all life on Earth emerged, and yet we know more about the surface of the Moon than we do about the sea floor. We are only just beginning to understand how complex this water world really is.

In this book, we'll journey across the globe from the warm coral seas of the tropics to the frozen oceans around the poles. Along the way, we'll meet a collection of creatures of all shapes, sizes and colors, and we'll learn about how they live and the challenges they face.

The oceans shape not only these creatures' lives but also our own. It is the oceans that regulate the weather and create the air that we breathe. So, as we discover the longest migration on Earth and visit its deepest seas, we'll also learn how our own actions affect the ocean, its inhabitants and our whole planet.

Ben Rothery

Red lionfish
Pterois volitans

FAMILIES

Around three quarters of all life on Earth lives in and around the oceans – an array that includes all the great classes of animals, and creatures of every shape, size and color imaginable. The sea and its surrounding shores are home to some of the most incredible species on Earth. In this section, we will meet some of them.

European spider crab
Maja squinado

Humpback whale
Megaptera novaeangliae

Leatherback turtle
Dermochelys coriacea

Atlantic puffin
Fratercula arctica

Chambered nautilus
Nautilus pompilius

Reptiles

A surprising number of reptiles dwell in our oceans. Cold-blooded, egg-laying and requiring air to breathe, most marine reptiles are tied to the land in one way or another. But a few – like the 69 species of sea snake – have shed this need and spend their entire lives at sea.

Of the others, some spend most of their lives in the water, but come ashore to lay their eggs – sea turtles and sea kraits are two examples. Others, including marine iguanas and saltwater crocodiles, live at least part of the time on land, but enter the water to find food or sanctuary.

Saltwater crocodile
Crocodylus porosus

Found in estuaries and coastal swamps throughout South East Asia and northern Australia, the saltwater crocodile is the largest reptile in the world. Newly hatched babies like this one measure around 28 centimeters (11 inches) long. but can grow to a massive 6 meters (20 feet).

Marine iguana
Amblyrhynchus cristatus

This species of lizard is found only on the Galapagos Islands, off the coast of Ecuador. Although most lizards are excellent swimmers, marine iguanas are unique in that they also forage in the sea for food such as algae.

Yellow-lipped sea krait
Laticauda colubrina

This venomous snake is found in tropical waters from the east coast of India to as far south as New Zealand. They spend most of their time hunting fish underwater, but must return to land to rest and reproduce.

Green sea turtle
Chelonia mydas

These large turtles are found in warm waters throughout the world and, despite their name, are actually olive or black. Thanks to their flattened bodies and large flippers, green sea turtles are strong swimmers. They migrate long distances – sometimes thousands of miles – between their feeding grounds and nesting beaches.

Mammals

There are five groups of marine mammals: pinnipeds (seals, sea lions, fur seals and walruses), cetaceans (whales, dolphins and porpoises), sirenians (dugongs and manatees), sea otters and polar bears. All breathe air, give birth to live young and – like all mammals – raise them on milk.

Of the five groups, only cetaceans and sirenians are fully aquatic, spending all of their lives in the water. Pinnipeds and sea otters give birth on land and return there for sanctuary, but spend most of their time in the water. Polar bears live and hunt on the frozen sea ice of the Arctic, entering the water only to feed.

Orca
Orcinus orca

The orca, or killer whale, is actually the largest member of the dolphin family. These highly intelligent hunters are found in every ocean. Orcas are apex predators, meaning they are at the very top of the ocean food chain: nothing eats them, and they are capable of hunting a diverse array of prey, from small fish to sharks and even whales.

Marine otter
Lontra felina

The marine otter is the smallest marine mammal, measuring between 87 and 115 centimeters (34 to 45 inches) from nose to tail and weighing less than 5 kilograms (11 pounds). Not much is known about this shy member of the weasel family, which is found along the Pacific coast of South America. With webbed feet, strong claws and some of the thickest fur in nature, the marine otter is superbly adapted to life in and around the sea.

Dugong
Dugong dugon

The dugong can be found grazing on seagrass across the Pacific Ocean, from the east coast of Africa to the west coast of Australia. It has a 3-meter-long (10-foot) body, paddle-shaped flippers and a dolphin-like tail, but is a slow swimmer and largely defenseless, so relies on its size for protection.

Southern elephant seal
Mirounga leonina

At nearly 6 meters (20 feet) long and weighing up to 4,000 kilograms, (8,800 pounds) the southern elephant seal is enormous. As well as being the largest member of the seal family and one of the largest carnivores alive today, this ocean giant is also the largest marine mammal that isn't a whale.

Fish

Fish are found in every part of the ocean, from the shallow waters of the tropics to the inky darkness of the deep sea. There are currently over 34,000 recognized species of fish, and likely many more, making them the most diverse group of vertebrates. Among them are some of the oldest species still alive today.

Most fish lay eggs, have scales and several sets of fins, and use a set of gills to extract oxygen from the water to breathe. Many fish are ectothermic, or cold-blooded, meaning their body temperature varies as temperatures around them change. However, there are some notable exceptions, which we'll meet as we go on.

Southern sunfish
Mola alexandrini

This unusual-looking fish is among the heaviest fish in the world – only basking sharks and whale sharks are heavier. Southern sunfish can be found relaxing on their sides across the warm southern Pacific and Indian oceans, and eat just about anything, including jellyfish. Oddly, sunfish don't have a tail, making them slow and awkward swimmers, but in spite of their clumsy appearance they are capable of moving fast and even of leaping out of the water when threatened.

Red gurnard
Chelidonichthys cuculus

Gurnards are little bottom-dwelling fish that feed
on smaller fish and crustaceans. They're commonly
known as sea robins, due to their red bellies and
large pectoral fins, which open and close like a
bird's wings when they swim.

Spotted eagle ray
Aetobatus narinari

At 3 meters (10 feet) wide and 5 meters (16 feet) long, spotted
eagle rays are the second-largest species of ray after manta rays.
These relatives of sharks can be found gliding through warm
waters across the world. They feed on shellfish and crustaceans
by crushing them with a bony plate that takes the place of teeth.
Spotted eagle rays defend themselves with two venomous spines
located on their tails, and they are famous for leaping over 2
meters (6.5 feet) into the air – although nobody knows why.

Copperband butterflyfish
Chelmon rostratus

The copperband butterflyfish is found
on coral reefs throughout the Indian
and Pacific oceans. It uses its long,
narrow nose and mouth to poke
into holes and crevices in the reef,
hunting for worms, brine shrimps
and other tiny crustaceans.

Arthropods

The largest and most diverse group of animals on the planet, arthropods account for over 80 per cent of all described living animals. They range in size from the tiny fairyfly – a wasp that measures around a millimeter in length – all the way up to the massive Japanese spider crab, which can measure up to 5.5 meters (18 feet) across.

There are three major groups of marine arthropod: crustaceans, sea spiders and horseshoe crabs. With roughly 30,000 species, crustaceans form the largest group of the three. As well as lobsters, crabs and shrimps, the crustacean family also includes barnacles and a whole range of tiny creatures, including amphipods, isopods and copepods. All arthropods share certain characteristics that make them unique from other families, the most obvious being their external skeleton, or exoskeleton, which protects them like a suit of armour.

European lobster
Homarus gammarus

These large crustaceans are found across the eastern Atlantic Ocean as well as the Mediterranean and Black seas. Like the closely related western Atlantic species *Homarus americanus*, they live from 20 to 50 years (or even more), and are among the biggest crustaceans – only the Japanese spider crab is larger. Lobsters are omnivorous, eating both plants and animals, such as fish and worms. They use large claws – one designed for crushing, and the other for cutting – to pull apart their food.

Arrow crab
Stenorhynchus seticornis

This brightly coloured crustacean with thin, spidery legs is found on coral reefs along the Atlantic coast of the Americas from the southern United States to Brazil. It gets its name from the shape of its body and head, which is triangular and tapers to a point, resembling an arrowhead.

Whale louse
Cyamidae

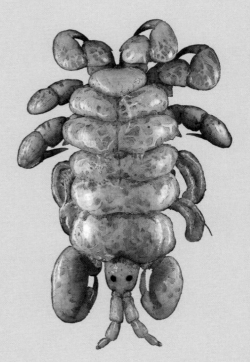

Whale lice are a family of approximately 31 species of tiny crustaceans, some measuring less than 5 millimeters (0.2 inch) in length. They spend their entire lives on the surface of whales, dolphins and porpoises, feeding on dead skin and algae. They cling to the folds and wrinkles on their hosts' bodies using three pairs of back legs that have developed into claws.

Mangrove horseshoe crab
Carcinoscorpius rotundicauda

These strange-looking arthropods are found in coastal swamps across South East Asia, and are actually more closely related to spiders or scorpions than they are to crabs. Horseshoe crabs have remained almost unchanged for over 400 million years, with fossil specimens looking almost identical to modern species.

Steller's sea eagle
Haliaeetus pelagicus

Birds

There are nearly 350 species of seabird, and almost as many birds again that are tied to the oceans in one way or another, including shorebirds, sea ducks, herons and sea eagles.

Seabirds vary enormously in lifestyle, behavior and size – from giant wanderers like the albatross to flightless underwater specialists like penguins – but they do share some similarities. Most species nest in colonies varying in size from a few dozen birds to millions. Seabirds often live longer and have fewer offspring than other birds, and sometimes spend as long as a year raising a single chick. Many seabirds undertake long annual migrations, crossing the equator or circumnavigating the Earth to breed or to find food. They feed at the ocean's surface and swim below it, putting to use a dazzling array of special features and behaviors.

Steller's sea eagle
Haliaeetus pelagicus

This massive eagle is found in coastal areas across north-eastern Asia, and is both the heaviest of all birds of prey and one of the largest. Fish make up roughly 80 per cent of its diet – it plucks them from the water with its sharp, hooked talons – but it will also prey upon waterbirds and small mammals, including baby seals.

Great cormorant
Phalacrocorax carbo

This large black seabird has webbed feet, a snakelike neck and a hooked beak. It is one of the most adaptable of all seabirds, and is found across the world, in a huge variety of habitats and temperature zones, from the Arctic to the tropics.

Piping plover
Charadrius melodus

The piping plover is a small shorebird found mainly along the eastern coastline of North America, where it breeds during spring and summer, before migrating down to the Caribbean in winter. Piping plovers can be hard to spot, as both the adults and chicks blend in well with the sand, and run in short bursts with frequent stops.

Little penguin
Eudyptula minor

The little penguin is found close to the coastlines of southern Australia and New Zealand, and is the smallest penguin species at only 33 centimeters (13 inches) tall. The largest – the emperor penguin – is more than four times taller and fifteen times heavier. Little penguins are quick and agile swimmers, and they hunt fish, squid and crustaceans.

Molluscs

Molluscs are the second most diverse and numerous family in the oceans, accounting for more than 23 per cent of all known marine species. They are found in all the world's oceans, with the smallest measuring less than 1 millimeter (0.04 inch) while the largest – the colossal and giant squids – can grow to over 15 meters (49 feet) long.

Variable
neon slug
Nembrotha kubaryana

There are seven classes of living molluscs, the three largest of which are gastropods, bivalves and cephalopods. Gastropods – which include sea snails and sea slugs – have a large foot that they use to crawl, and usually have a one-piece shell that is typically spiralled. Bivalves – such as clams, oysters and mussels – have a two-part shell that can open and close. Cephalopods are intelligent animals with well-developed brains, and include species like octopus, cuttlefish and squid. Many cephalopods are efficient predators and have some impressive adaptations to help them hunt, including camouflage and the ability to change their color and body shape.

Coconut octopus
Amphioctopus marginatus

The coconut octopus is found in warm waters across South East Asia. It gets its name from its habit of climbing inside the two halves of a coconut, and then pulling the pieces together to hide. Like its distant relative the flamboyant cuttlefish, the coconut octopus also prefers to use its arms to walk along the sea floor – often carrying its favorite coconut along with it.

20

Variable neon slug
Nembrotha kubaryana

The variable neon slug is a large, colorful species also known as a nudibranch, after the scientific name Nudibranchia, which means 'naked gills' – a reference to the feathery gills that many members of the species have on their backs. There are more than 2,000 known species of nudibranch spread throughout the world, but most live in shallow tropical waters.

Princely cone snail
Conus aulicus

Cone snails are a group of over 600 species of venomous, predatory sea snails found in warm waters worldwide. These harmless-looking snails prey upon small fish, worms and even other cone snails. Although blind, they are able to sense when their prey is nearby, then attack with a venomous modified tooth called a toxoglossan radula.

Flamboyant cuttlefish
Metasepia pfefferi

This brightly colored cuttlefish is found mainly in the tropical waters between Australia and the Philippines. Unlike most of its swimming relatives, the flamboyant cuttlefish prefers to walk along the sea floor using two of its arms – this action is known as 'ambling'. While other cuttlefish squirt ink when threatened, the flamboyant cuttlefish flashes colors and patterns designed to startle or hypnotize its predators, allowing it to slip away.

LIFE IN MINIATURE

The most important organisms in the world's oceans are also the smallest: plankton. These microscopic organisms are the foundation of the ocean's entire food web. Their presence dictates why everything else lives where it does – and it's because of plankton that anything lives at all.

Their name comes from the Greek word *planktos*, meaning 'drifter', which is precisely what plankton are: they neither stay in one place nor swim on their own, instead drifting on the ocean's currents and tides. There are two main types of plankton: phytoplankton (which is made up of tiny plants and algae) and zooplankton (tiny animals, including the eggs and larval stages of many larger species, such as fish, crustaceans and even coral).

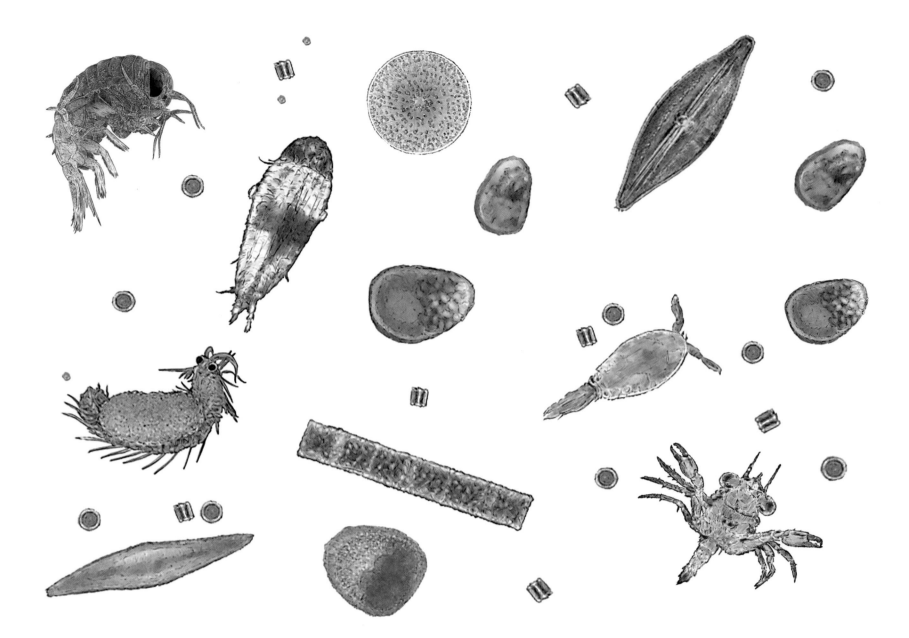

Phytoplankton create energy through a process called photosynthesis, using the natural pigment chlorophyll and sunlight. Like other plants, phytoplankton absorb the greenhouse gas carbon dioxide and release oxygen. In fact, phytoplankton are the most important producer of oxygen on Earth, accounting for about half of the photosynthesis on the planet – that's more than all the world's forests combined.

Zooplankton and other small marine creatures such as krill eat phytoplankton, then become in turn food for larger species, even some whales.

Climate change and rising sea temperatures pose a serious threat to plankton in all of the world's oceans. This matters not only because the entire marine food chain depends on plankton, but also because these minuscule creatures play such an important role in creating the oxygen we breathe. Plankton are essential for both healthy water worlds and the planet as a whole.

Open ocean

Far from land lies the open ocean, an unimaginably large habitat covering more than 360 million cubic kilometers (86 million cubic miles) and stretching from the sun-dappled waters at the surface to the lightless and ice-cold depths near the sea floor. In this huge expanse of water there are hundreds of deserted miles, punctuated with little pockets of life. Sea creatures pass through on their way to breeding or feeding grounds. Floating debris provides temporary shelter for juvenile fish, and also acts as a homing beacon for predators and giants lurking far below.

In this section, we'll meet some of the hunters that patrol the open seas, and those that seek to avoid these predators. Here, you will find whales, sharks, giant jellyfish and immense shoals of tiny fish engaged in an endless game of cat and mouse.

Blue shark
Prionace glauca

Found in deep waters across the world, the blue shark is well adapted for life in the open ocean. Its blue-and-white coloration is a form of camouflage called countershading, and is useful for a hunter in an environment with no cover – the sleek blue blends in with the water below, and the shark's white belly blends in with the sunlight reflecting on the ocean's surface.

Pilot fish
Naucrates ductor

Pilot fish have a mutualistic relationship with sharks, rays and various other predators, meaning both species benefit from the relationship. Pilot fish gain protection from their hosts in exchange for keeping the predator free of parasites.

Blue shark *(Prionace glauca)* and
pilot fish *(Naucrates ductor)*

The oceans

The ocean is an enormous, interconnected habitat that covers approximately 71 per cent of the Earth's surface, contains 97 per cent of its water and has an average depth of nearly 3,700 meters (12,000 feet).

It is divided into the five great oceans, in descending order by size Pacific, Atlantic, Indian, Antarctic and Arctic, and a number of different regions on either side of the equator, an imaginary line that stretches round the middle of the Earth halfway between the North Pole and South Pole, where the planet is at its widest.

In this section we will learn about where these oceans lie in relation to one another and about what happens at the different depths that make up this massive and varied habitat.

Climate zones

This map shows the three major climate zones on Earth: polar, temperate and tropical. The polar regions are the coldest, the tropical regions are the warmest, and the temperate regions are neither very cold nor very warm.

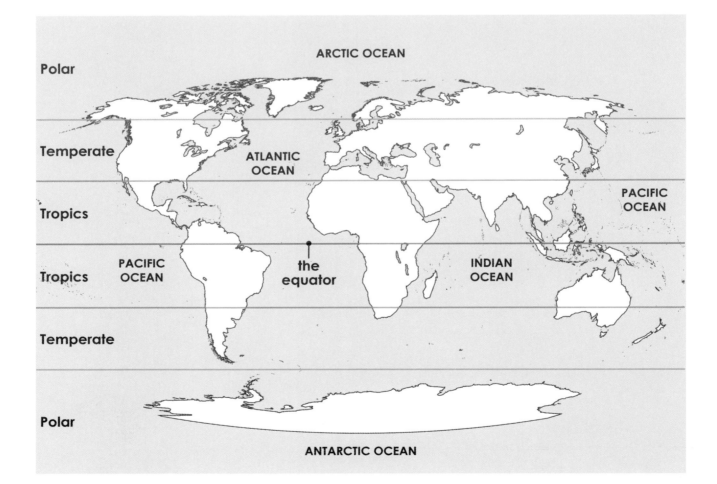

A) Intertidal zone

An area of constant change containing the high and low tidelines, beaches, rockpools, mangroves and swamps.

B) Coastal / inshore waters

Light and shallow, inshore waters teem with life and contain a range of habitats, including coral reefs, forests of kelp and plains of seagrasses.

C) Open ocean

In the spaces between land lies the open ocean; the world's largest biome is deep and sparsely populated.

Land **A** **B** **C**

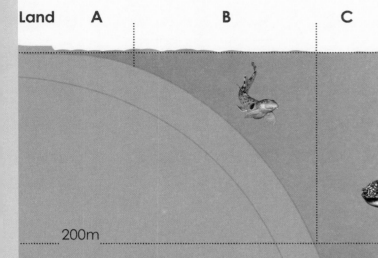

200m

D) Sunlight zone (euphotic)

These are the sunlit waters from the surface down to a depth of about 200 meters (650 feet). Most of the ocean's life is found here, it is where photosynthesis takes place and where large ocean hunters like swordfish and marlin prowl.

E) Twilight zone (dysphotic)

The sun's light only reaches very weakly into the waters of the twilight zone and towards the bottom of it almost not at all. But these waters still teem with living things, some of which live here permanently and others like the giant ocean sunfish that visit to feed before returning to the warmer waters near the surface.

1,000m

F) Midnight zone (aphotic)

No light at all reaches the waters of the midnight zone. It is a world of perpetual darkness and is sparsely populated compared to the waters above.

Ocean habitats

This diagram shows different zones within an ocean. The depth and movement of the water changes from zone to zone, and so does the amount of light and warmth from the Sun.

G) Seabed

Striped marlin *(Kajikia audax)* feeding on
Pacific mackerel *(Scomber japonicus)*

Striped marlin
Kajikia audax

Striped marlin can grow to over 3 meters (10 feet) in length and are some of the fastest fish in the sea, capable of bursts of speed of up to 80 kilometers (50 miles) per hour.

Marlin rely on their large eyes to hunt, and patrol near the water's surface, where it's well lit. When they become excited, marlin change color and light up with iridescent blue stripes that confuse their prey to make it easier to catch. They slash at their prey – such as the Pacific mackerel – with their long bills, injuring and stunning it, before coming back to collect it.

Out in the open ocean, with nowhere to hide, a Pacific mackerel's only defense is to gather into a tight ball with the rest of its shoal. Any single fish will be quickly caught. At least within the shoal there is safety in numbers.

Deep seas

The deep sea is the largest and one of the most hostile environments on Earth. It is an alien world of bitter cold, crushing pressure and total darkness, but it is also home to more life than anywhere else in the ocean. The twilight zone – the lowest level of the ocean that light can reach – is home to 90 per cent of all the fish in the ocean.

Survival here means making the most of every glimmer of light and every scrap of food, as finding a meal can be hard and finding a mate even harder. The creatures that live here have adapted in many ways. Some have huge eyes to see in the dull waters. There are fish that walk rather than swim, creatures with transparent heads, and animals that light up. Here, all manner of fins, spines, lures and tentacles can be found.

Life in the deep

Some creatures that live in the deep sea are found nowhere else, while others simply pass through to hunt or hide – or both – before returning to the lighter waters above. The deeper you go, the more extreme the conditions and the creatures become. Light is a distant memory, and the weight of the water above creates pressure that would crush most surface-dwellers.

Sperm whales spend most of their time near the ocean's surface, but descend into the deep to hunt. Measuring up to 20 meters (65 feet) in length and weighing as much as 45 metric tons (100,000 pounds), these huge whales undertake 90-minute dives of up to 2 kilometers (1.25 miles) – on one breath – to do battle with giant squid in the frozen darkness. Giant squid, by contrast, spend their whole lives in the deep ocean. These massive cephalopods grow up to 13 meters (43 feet) long and are superbly adapted to life in the almost lightless depths, with the largest eyes in the animal kingdom. Measuring 25 centimeters (10 inches) across, these huge eyes enable the squid to detect prey where most other creatures would see nothing. Even the squid's red coloring is a type of camouflage – red light doesn't penetrate to the ocean's depths, meaning that red creatures actually appear black, making them invisible to predators and prey.

Mauve stinger (*Pelagia noctiluca*)

Deep-sea anglerfish
Diceratias pileatus

There are over 200 species of anglerfish. They can be found in all the world's oceans, but most live in the depths of the Atlantic and the Antarctic oceans, up to a mile down. These carnivores have huge heads and enormous crescent-shaped mouths filled with sharp, translucent teeth. Anglerfish can range in size from 2 centimeters to 1 meter (0.8 inch to 39 inches), with females being the largest.

Anglerfish get their name from their most distinctive feature, which is found only on the female: a long spine tipped with a lump of glowing flesh that protrudes past the mouth like a fishing rod. Using this rod, a female anglerfish lures prey close enough to snatch it. Her mouth is so big and her body so flexible that she can swallow prey up to twice her own size, including snails and small fish.

Hydrothermal vents

More than three quarters of the planet's volcanic activity occurs in the very deepest parts of the ocean. Cracks form along the edges of tectonic plates – the giant sheets of rock that make up the Earth's crust – and allow seawater to seep in. When that water comes into contact with hot magma below the Earth's surface, it is super-heated into gas and hot liquid. This gushes through gaps in the rock and, over time, minerals deposited from these jets form immense stacks known as hydrothermal vents.

Shrimp, hairy crabs and giant tube worms cover every inch of these vents. It was in a place just like this that it is thought life on Earth first began, four billion years ago. Cut off from the energy of the sun, these ecosystems depend entirely on bacteria for their food. The bacteria feed on the chemicals belched from the vents, and in turn provide sustenance for the incredible diversity of life.

Hydrothermal vents are thought to hold as much life as tropical rainforests. As many as half a million individual animals can be found in a single square metre, and some are unique to a particular vent and found nowhere else. On average, a new species has been discovered every ten days since these ecosystems were unearthed in 1977.

Vent eelpout
Thermarces cerberus

Yeti crab
Kiwa hirsuta

35

Manta ray
Mobula alfredi

ISLANDS

Islands provide refuge, both above and below the waves, for many animals and plants. These remote outposts pepper the world's oceans, offering stopping points for wanderers and permanent homes for others.

Islands are as diverse as they are numerous. Giants like Madagascar, off the coast of East Africa, contain rainforests and deserts, and boast an incredible collection of animal and plant castaways. On Madagascar, you will find species that have evolved in isolation over millions of years, 90 per cent of which are not found anywhere else.

In contrast are desolate places like Bouvet Island, a frozen outcrop adrift in the Antarctic Ocean. At more than 1,600 kilometers (990 miles) in any direction from the nearest land, it is the most remote island in the world. But even a place as unforgiving as this provides a haven for many forms of life, including hundreds of thousands of nesting seabirds and seals.

Without the sanctuary that islands provide, some of the most remarkable species alive today simply wouldn't exist. Evolving and adapting in isolation can lead to an animal being superbly suited to its environment – but it can also mean that animal is more vulnerable to change than species on the mainland.

Blue-footed booby
Sula nebouxii

Nesting and breeding

Islands provide a venue for many of the ocean's inhabitants to meet, find a mate and raise their young. These isolated land masses – which are sometimes hundreds of miles from the nearest mainland – create focal points for life in the otherwise empty expanse of the open ocean. All over the world, seabirds, seals and sea lions gather to breed in vast island colonies, safe from land-based predators.

And it's not just the safety that islands offer which makes them such attractive places to breed. Creatures of all kinds come for another key reason: food. Far below the water's surface, vast and deep ocean currents collide with the sides of an island and are driven upwards. These currents bring with them rich nutrients that in turn attract huge concentrations of life, providing a ready food source for both residents and visitors, and are particularly important for creatures raising their young.

Blue-footed booby
Sula nebouxii

These marine birds nest along the western coast of the Americas, from the Gulf of California to South America, but over half of all breeding pairs gather in huge colonies on the Galapagos Islands in the eastern Pacific Ocean.

Their name comes from the Spanish word *bobo*, meaning 'clown', in reference to their clumsy movement on land, but they're graceful in the air and below the water. Boobies fly far out to sea, searching for schools of small fish such as anchovies, which they catch by diving. Folding their long wings back round their bodies, they plunge into the water from heights of 20 meters (65 feet) or more.

Ring-tailed lemur
Lemur catta

Magical Madagascar

The safety and remoteness of some islands make them the ideal spot for creatures to change over time into forms found nowhere else. As a result, these islands become home to all sorts of weird and wonderful species.

One of these exceptional islands is Madagascar, which is in the Indian Ocean and is home to more unique species than any other island in the world. Around 15,000 of the plants and animals found there exist nowhere else on Earth – that includes lemurs, tenrecs and more than half of the world's species of chameleon.

The incredible diversity of life found on Madagascar is partly due to the island's size, and partly due to its extreme age. The island was formed nearly 90 million years ago, when it broke away from East Africa, meaning the wildlife has had a long time to adapt in its own way. It is also the fourth-largest island in the world, and has many different habitats for species to live in.

Ring-tailed lemurs are found only on Madagascar. Their primate ancestors washed up on the arid west coast of the island, and evolved over thousands of years into the form we see today. They live together in troops of up to 30, and spend most of their time foraging in the forest for a wide variety of plants.

For millions of years, Madagascar's unique wildlife evolved slowly and in isolation. However, since humans arrived roughly 10,000 years ago, the pace of change to the environment has become faster than many animals can cope with. As little as 20 per cent of the island's original forest remains, and many species now face extinction, including almost all 105 species of lemur.

Record-breakers

The ocean is home to some of the most impressive species on Earth. Here, we'll meet some watery record-breakers, including the fastest fish in the sea, the animal that undertakes the longest migration on our planet, and the largest creature alive.

LARGEST SPECIES:
Blue whale (*Balaenoptera musculus*)

At 30 meters (98 feet) long and weighing as much as 190 metric tons (420,000 pounds), the blue whale is not only the largest animal on Earth, but also the largest animal known to have ever existed.

FASTEST IN THE SEA:
Atlantic sailfish (*Istiophorus albicans*)

With a top speed of nearly 115 kilometers (71 miles) per hour, the sailfish is widely considered the fastest fish in the world.

STRONGEST BITE:
Saltwater crocodile (*Crocodylus porosus*)

As well as being the largest living reptile, the saltwater crocodile also has the strongest bite force of any animal. Their jaws are almost twice as powerful as those of a great white shark.

LOUDEST ANIMAL:
Sperm whale (*Physeter macrocephalus*)

Sperm whales are capable of making short sounds at a volume of 230 decibels – louder than a rocket launch or a fighter jet at take-off. These sounds can be heard by other whales thousands of miles away.

LONGEST-LIVING VERTEBRATE:
Greenland shark (*Somniosus microcephalus*)

The rarely seen Greenland shark holds the record for the longest-living vertebrate, with a lifespan of at least 500 years – around seven times that of an average human.

LONGEST MIGRATION:
Arctic tern (*Sterna paradisaea*)

Flying between the Arctic and the Antarctic each year, the Arctic tern holds the record for the longest migration, with an annual round trip of more than 64,000 kilometers (40,000 miles). Spending summer in both poles means that the Arctic tern also sees more daylight than any other animal.

Whale shark

Rhincodon typus

Often growing to over 18 meters (59 feet) long,
the whale shark is the largest fish in the sea. These
gentle giants are found close to the surface in
tropical waters all around the world. In spite of their
enormous size, they are harmless to most creatures,
as they feed almost exclusively on plankton and tiny fish.

TEMPERATE SEAS

The temperate seas stretch round the Earth in two massive bands between the icy waters of the poles and the warmer waters of the tropics. These relatively shallow seas are some of the richest on the planet.

Leopard shark
Triakis semifasciata

Warm tropical water moving north and south towards the poles mixes with cold polar water moving towards the equator, and sucks up nutrients from the seabed. These nutrients support enormous quantities of plankton, which in turn attract huge shoals of fish, whales, sharks, seals, sea lions and more.

Many ocean fish start their lives in temperate waters, sheltering in kelp forests or drifting on the currents among the zooplankton.

California sea lion
Zalophus californianus

The California sea lion is quick, reaching speeds of up to 40 kilometers (25 miles) per hour as it pursues the fish, squid and shellfish that make up most of its diet. Unlike most seals, which are awkward on land, sea lions can stand up on their front flippers and rotate their hind ones forward to use all four limbs when moving around out of the water.

Male California sea lions have large bumps on their heads, and lack the distinctive lion-like manes that give other sea lions their name. They are brilliantly adapted for swimming, with a streamlined body and powerful flippers, as well as a thick layer of blubber to insulate them from the cold.

Kelp forests

Along the margins of the temperate seas lie the forests of the ocean. Here, sunlight powers the growth of massive kelp – a green-brown seaweed – forests that cover around a quarter of the planet's coastlines. Kelp is a type of seaweed with a long, tough stalk and broad fronds divided into strips.

Off the tip of southern Africa, where the South Atlantic and Indian oceans collide, the rich waters support nearly a hundred different species of shark, including the great white.

These fearsome hunters are drawn to the glades and edges of the underwater kelp forests by the vast shoals of fish, and by the colonies of seals and seabirds that feed on them.

Further north, on the Pacific coast of North America, lie the largest kelp forests on Earth. They stretch for hundreds of miles and grow as tall as 60 meters (200 feet). Here, sea stars, Garibaldi fish and sea otters battle huge swarms of spiny sea urchins, which graze on the roots of the kelp and, if left unchecked, can completely destroy a forest.

Sea otter
Enhydra lutris

Sea otters gather in groups along the Pacific coasts of North America and Asia. They spend a lot of their time in the water, but occasionally come ashore to sleep or rest. Sea otters mostly float on their backs, and even sleep like this, sometimes 'holding hands' with each other so that they don't drift as they doze.

In the kelp forests, sea otters wrap the seaweed round themselves to provide an anchor in the ocean's swell. This enables them to engage in a fascinating behavior. Lying on its back, the sea otter will place a rock on its chest, then repeatedly smash its shellfish and sea-urchin prey against the rock until the shell breaks open and the otter can get at the food inside.

Unlike most marine mammals, which have a thick layer of blubber to keep them warm, the sea otter's primary form of insulation is an exceptionally thick coat of fur – the densest in the animal kingdom. Otters were once hunted almost to the point of extinction for this fur coat, and by the early twentieth century fewer than 2,000 animals remained. Today, sea otters are protected by law, and their numbers have started to recover.

Great white shark

Carcharodon carcharias

Found in cool, coastal waters throughout the world, great white sharks are the largest predatory fish. They grow to an average of 4.5 meters (15 feet) long, but females can reach over 6 meters (20 feet) and weigh as much as 2.5 metric tons (5,500 pounds). The great white's main prey includes seals, sea lions, small whales and sea turtles, although it will take advantage of any meal, including the floating carcasses of dead whales.

The great white hunts in temperate waters, with its countershaded deep-grey upper body making it almost invisible to its prey above.

Its streamlined body and powerful tail enable it to reach speeds of up to 56 kilometers (35 miles) per hour, and it sometimes leaves the water completely in a behaviour known as 'breaching'.

Displaying a fearsome smile, the great white's jaw is lined with as many as 300 serrated triangular teeth. These teeth are arranged in several rows so that, as the ones at the front become damaged, they're replaced by the ones behind. Great white sharks also have an excellent sense of smell, and are able to detect a single drop of blood in billions of drops of water.

Epaulette shark
Hemiscyllium ocellatum

COASTLINES

Along the Earth's coastlines, two worlds collide to create a complex and varied array of habitats. Ranging from sandy beaches to mangrove swamps, and bare rock to coral reef, each habitat has its unique challenges and cast of characters.

On the beach, turtles haul themselves up the sand to lay their eggs in the same place where they hatched many years earlier. Seabirds, seals and sea lions come to land to breed, while crabs scavenge in rock pools, and wading birds pick through the debris abandoned by the tide.

At Australia's Great Barrier Reef, low tide turns parts of the exposed reef into a series of rock pools, forcing larger hunters into deeper water and creating an opportunity for smaller ones like the epaulette shark. These little sharks have evolved the ability to walk, using their fins like legs to crawl between rock pools in search of food. No shark can breathe out of water, but the epaulette shark is able to survive for up to an hour without oxygen by slowing its breathing and heart rate to an almost complete standstill. This gives the shark time to hunt on the reef before the tide comes back in, bringing their larger cousins with it.

Bengal tiger
Panthera tigris tigris

Mangrove forests

The mangrove forest is one of the richest coastal habitats on Earth, and is found all over the world. Straddling the margin between the land and tropical sea, this space provides a nursery for juvenile fish and acts as a barrier, protecting the coast from damage by strong waves and storms.

The mangrove forest is made up of specially adapted mangrove shrubs, which are capable of surviving in salty water with their extensive, exposed root system. As well as helping the tree to store gases from the air, the mangrove's roots also provide shelter for shrimp, crabs, molluscs and various fish, including young barracuda and small sharks. Sheltered among the roots, the fish can develop into adults before moving into the open ocean. In fact, approximately one third of all marine fish species spend part of their lives in mangrove forests.

The Sundarbans is the world's largest mangrove forest, covering more than 10,000 square kilometers (3,850 square miles) of Bangladesh and north-west India, and it's here that we find perhaps the most surprising mangrove inhabitant: the Bengal tiger. This tiger has adapted to its environment and exhibits a range of unusual behaviors that separate it from other tiger populations. It climbs trees and preys on crabs and fish, swims at speeds of up to 13 kilometers (8 miles) per hour – even against strong tides and currents – and can drink salty water that its land-living relatives cannot.

Mudskippers (*Oxudercidae*)

Mudskippers are funny little fish that can survive both in and out of the water. There are 32 species, and they are found in tropical, subtropical and temperate regions, from Indonesia to the west coast of Africa.

One of the mudskipper's most noticeable features is its side pectoral fins, which are located towards the front of its body. The fish uses these fins like legs to walk, climb trees and even 'skip' distances of up to 60 centimeters (24 inches) across muddy surfaces – hence its name.

Great blue-spotted mudskipper
Boleophthalmus pectinirostris

British Columbia wolf

Canis lupus columbianus

In the westernmost part of Canada there exists a unique population of coastal wolves that live almost entirely off the sea. The British Columbia wolf is about 20 per cent smaller than its inland grey wolf cousin, and as much as 90 per cent of its diet is fish, seafood and marine mammals, rather than the more typical elk or deer favored by other wolves. It is also capable of swimming up to 12 kilometers (7.5 miles) between islands in search of food.

TROPICAL SEAS

The warm, shallow waters around the equator are home to an abundance of life. Brightly colored fish cluster around coral reefs, competing for space and sheltering from the sharks patrolling the reef's edge. Sea turtles graze on vast plains of seagrass that stretch as far as the eye can see. Humpback whales travel huge distances from their feeding grounds in colder waters to mate or give birth, leaving after a few short weeks in search of more plentiful food – these giant wanderers are found in every ocean on Earth.

West Indian manatee
Trichechus manatus

Weighing up to 600 kilograms (1,300 pounds), the West Indian manatee inhabits warm, coastal waters, including rivers and estuaries, from the southern United States to as far south as Brazil. Moving slowly through the mangroves, it spends as much as half of its time asleep. The manatee's closest relative is the elephant, but it is also known as the sea cow, because it's a slow, peaceful plant-eater that lives in herds and grazes on water plants.

Tiger shark
Galeocerdo cuvier

Tiger sharks are found in tropical and subtropical waters. They can grow to over 7 meters (23 feet) long and weigh nearly 900 kilograms (2,000 pounds). They have excellent senses, and powerful jaws filled with sharp serrated teeth that allow them to tackle a range of prey, from sea turtles to sea snakes. These fearsome hunters, sometimes called 'the ocean's garbage can', will eat absolutely anything – the stomach contents of captured sharks have been found to include car license plates and tires.

Coral reefs

Although they occupy less than 1 per cent of the ocean floor, coral reefs are home to a quarter of all known marine species. Beautiful and complex, coral reefs start from small beginnings – floating coral larvae attach to hard coastal surfaces, then over hundreds of years grow into spectacularly colorful structures.

Although they appear to be brightly colored rock, each coral is actually made up of hundreds or even thousands of tiny creatures called polyps. Each individual polyp is around 1.5 centimeters (0.6 inch) long, but together these polyps create incredible structures so large that they can be seen from outer space.

However, despite their size, coral reefs are under increasing pressure due to climate change and issues such as rising ocean temperatures. Coral is so colorful because of tiny algae called zooxanthellae, which provide the coral with food. These algae benefit from the coral as a home, but even an increase in the ocean's temperature of less than 1 degree Celsius causes the coral to force out the algae, leaving the coral bleached. If the temperature remains high, the coral won't let the algae back in, and both will die.

Dragon moray eel
Enchelycore pardalis

There are more than 200 species of the snakelike moray eel found in oceans the world over. Moray eels spend most of their time hidden in crevices on reefs, ready to attack any fish or crustacean unlucky enough to pass within reach. They have powerful jaws filled with sharp, backwards-facing teeth, as well as a second set of jaws housed in their throats, creating a very unfortunate situation for captured prey.

The reef edge

At the edge of every coral reef lies the drop-off, where the protective shelter of the reef falls away and there is nowhere to hide, particularly at night when sharks come out to hunt.

Species such as the silvertip, grey and blacktip reef shark play a major role in shaping and managing coral-reef communities. As the top predators, these sharks help to maintain the delicate balance of marine life by preying on fish species that graze the reef, and on smaller predators that would otherwise strip the reef of smaller species. Without sharks, the health of the whole marine ecosystem suffers.

However, these marine predators are vulnerable to the most dangerous hunter of all: humans. Each year, many thousands of sharks are caught for their meat and fins, or injured or killed by commercial fishing for other species. Since sharks are a large, slow-breeding species that only gives birth to a few live young each year, their populations cannot replenish at the same rate as they are caught by humans.

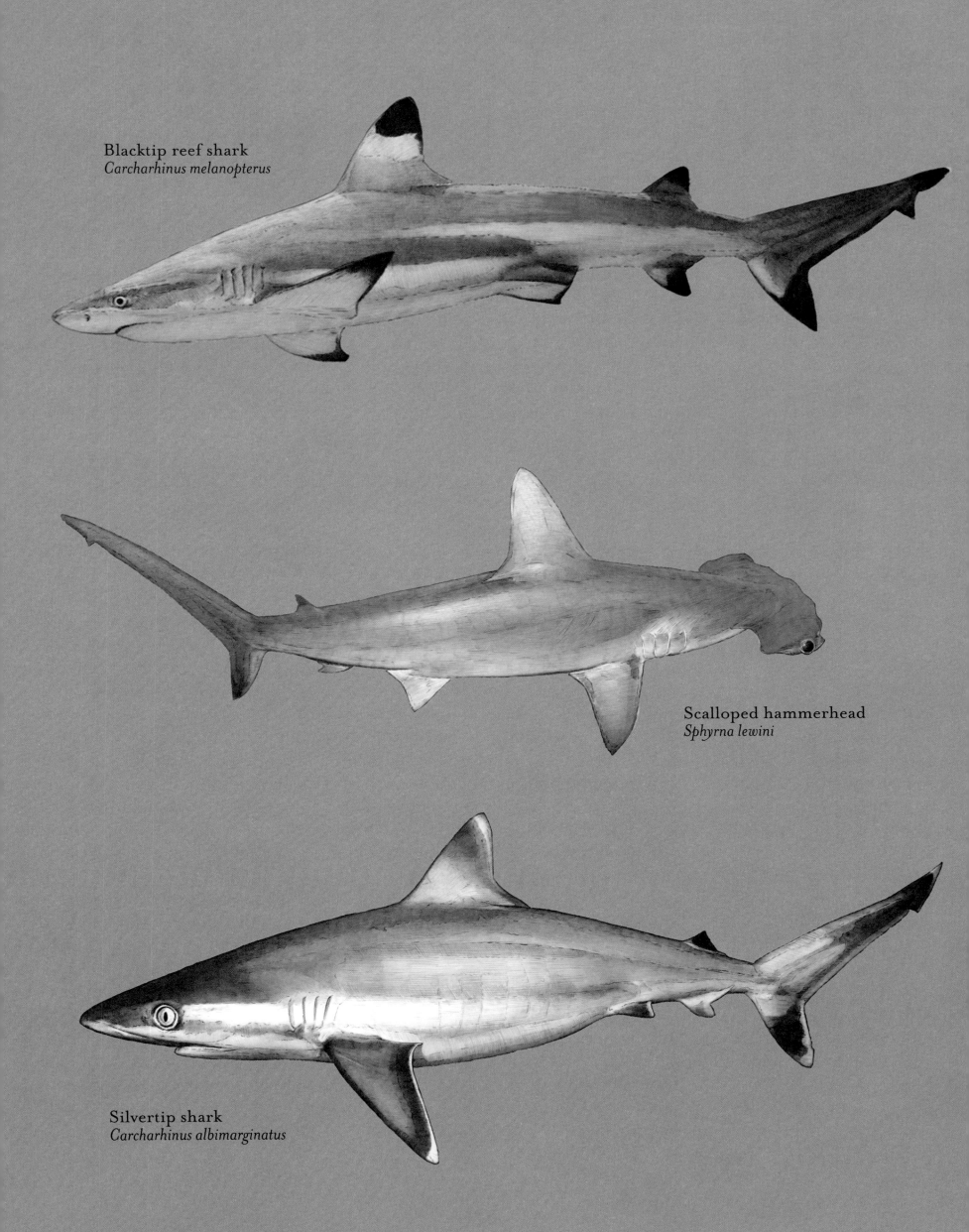

Blacktip reef shark
Carcharhinus melanopterus

Scalloped hammerhead
Sphyrna lewini

Silvertip shark
Carcharhinus albimarginatus

WEIRD AND WONDERFUL

Earth's water world is home to some of our planet's strangest animals – creatures so alien in their appearance and abilities as to seem otherworldly. Some differ wildly from the rest of their species, while others are one of a kind. There are animals that look like seaweed or stones, and creatures that can glow in the dark or change their body shape entirely. We'll meet fish that live on land and others that can fly, as well as living fossils and creatures found nowhere else on Earth.

Yellow seahorse
Hippocampus kuda

Seahorses are found in warm, shallow seas around the world. With its upright body and small fins, the yellow seahorse is a weak swimmer, so it uses its tail to anchor itself to seaweed, coral and seagrass, and simply waits for its food – such as plankton and small shrimps – to drift by.

Unlike most other fish, seahorses mate for life, and are one of the few species where the male, rather than the female, carries the unborn young. The male has a pouch on his belly, where the female lays her eggs. The male then fertilizes the eggs internally, and carries them until they hatch as fully formed, miniature versions of their parents.

Blue dragon nudibranch
Glaucus atlanticus

This species of small, predatory, ocean-going molluscs mainly feeds on jellyfish. They then store their prey's stinging cells within their own bodies as a defense against predators.

Flying fish
Exocoetidae

Flying fish live in all the oceans, and particularly in warm tropical waters. There are about 64 species, all of which have a unique ability: they can fly. However, flying fish do not fly in the same way as birds do. Instead, they are able to launch themselves out of the water, then their long fins – like wings – enable them to glide for considerable distances above the water's surface.

The main reason flying fish do this is to escape from predators. When they take to the air, they are capable of speeds of more than 60 kilometers (37 miles) per hour, covering distances of up to 400 meters (1,300 feet).

Tropical two-wing flying fish
Exocoetus volitans

65

Bigfin reef squid

Sepioteuthis lessoniana

Bigfin reef squid are found all over the world, in tropical and temperate waters such as the Indian and the Pacific oceans. They range in length from 4 to 33 centimeters (1.5 to 13 inches), and reach their full size in only four months, making them the fastest-growing of any large marine invertebrate (an animal without a spine). Bigfin reef squid can rapidly change their body's color and pattern at will, usually for camouflage to hide from predators and prey. The surface of their body also reflects different kinds of light to create all sorts of metallic blues, greens and reds. These shimmery colors are called iridescence.

Arctic tern
Sterna paradisaea

FROZEN SEAS

The Arctic and Antarctic oceans

At the top and bottom of the Earth lie the polar regions: the Arctic Ocean in the north, and the Antarctic Ocean in the south. These frozen wastelands are among the harshest environments on the planet. Although bitterly cold, both regions are technically deserts, with very little rainfall. Even so, life persists here.

It is thought that approximately 13,000 species call these seas home. Surviving at the ends of the Earth is difficult. Icy winds whip across the landscape, temperatures drop far below freezing, and in winter the darkness can last for months. Yet these seemingly barren landscapes are home to a rich diversity of life, both on land and under the water – life that has evolved to survive in the harshest conditions.

Polar animals have many adaptations that help them to survive in the extreme cold: warm fur, thick blubber (fat) and even a special antifreeze in their blood to stop it from freezing. These features enable them to thrive in conditions that would prove deadly to other animals.

Narwhal

Monodon monoceros

Also known as the unicorn of the sea, the narwhal is actually a close relative of the dolphin, and is found across the Arctic Circle. The narwhal's spiralling tusk, which can grow to over 3 meters (10 feet) long, is actually one of its teeth and grows through its upper lip. Until recently, nobody was quite sure what narwhals used these tusks for, but new observations show that they are used for hunting. Narwhals typically travel in groups of around fifteen, but sometimes gather in the hundreds to feed on fish and squid.

Animals of the frozen world

More than 200 species can be found in both polar regions. One example is the Arctic tern *(Sterna paradisaea)*, a tiny bird that weighs a little over 100 grams (about the same as a banana), but undertakes the longest migration on Earth. Every year, Arctic terns fly more than 64,000 kilometres on the round trip between the Arctic and the Antarctic. They make this migration in order to spend the summer at each of the two poles, and as a result they experience more daylight than any other animal on Earth.

The polar regions of our planet may seem too far away for humans to have much of an impact on them. However, even the things we do thousands of miles away – such as burning fossil fuels or throwing away plastic that will never disappear – can negatively affect these areas. We are changing these frozen worlds, and these changes affect the planet as a whole. Although the polar regions are so remote and so cold, it is these areas that feel most keenly the effects of global warming (the rise of the Earth's temperature) – both the Arctic and the Antarctic are warming up to three times faster than the average for the rest of the world.

The sea ice that covers these oceans provides both a refuge and a hunting ground for animals such as polar bears, walruses, seals and penguins. The ice spreads in winter, then in summer up to half its volume melts away. But that summer ice cover is shrinking because of rising temperatures, which puts an enormous amount of pressure on the animals that depend on it for their survival. Sadly, the very adaptations that allow creatures like polar animals to survive where others can't also mean that they are ill-equipped to deal with relatively rapid changes to their environment. If the sea ice disappears, so too will these animals.

The polar bear (*Ursus maritimus*) lives primarily in the Arctic Circle. The male can weigh up to 700 kilograms (1,500 pounds), but the female is much smaller at around half that size. A polar bear eats mostly seals, which it hunts around the sea ice, and this is why it is considered a marine mammal.

King penguin

Aptenodytes patagonicus

Standing at nearly a meter (3 feet) tall and weighing as much as 15 kilograms (33 pounds), the king penguin is the second-largest penguin species after the emperor. King penguins are found throughout the Antarctic, both on the continent and its surrounding islands.

King penguins feed mainly on fish and squid, which they catch far out at sea, before returning to land to rest. They also breed onshore, each pair raising two chicks every three years in vast colonies. Their only predator is the leopard seal, although the brown skua seabird will sometimes attack their chicks.

Leopard seal

Hydrurga leptonyx

Sea leopards are highly intelligent, with large heads, powerful jaws and long muscular bodies. They grow to a length of 3.5 meters (11.5 feet) and weigh in at 600 kilograms (1,300 pounds), and have counter-shaded skin, making them excellent hunters. They are capable of tackling a wide variety of prey, including birds, fish and even other seals.

King penguin and chick
Aptenodytes patagonicus

Pacific walrus

Odobenus rosmarus divergens

At over 3 meters (10 feet) long and weighing over a metric ton (2,200 pounds), the Pacific walrus is one of the largest pinnipeds – only the elephant seal is larger.

The Pacific walrus has a wrinkled brown body, large flat flippers, grizzled whiskers and thick, insulating blubber. Its long white tusks can grow to nearly a meter (3 feet) long, and the walrus uses them for a variety of tasks, including hauling its huge body out of the water and breaking breathing holes into the ice from below. It also uses its tusks to defend itself against predators such as polar bears and orcas, and the males use theirs to fight one another for territory during mating season.

Dear Reader,

The oceans are the Earth's last great wilderness, and we must take urgent steps to protect them. If we don't, then many of the iconic species you have seen in this book will disappear within a generation, along with other species we've yet even to discover.

Our water world is under threat like never before. It is changing faster than at any time in human history. This is in part because our climate is changing and, with it, the stable conditions that have allowed life to flourish for millions of years.

Climate change, ocean acidification, overfishing and plastic pollution are having a disastrous impact on the health of marine systems the world over. There has never been a more urgent need to learn about what goes on beneath the waves than now. The more that we understand our oceans and the creatures that rely on them, the better we will appreciate the fragility of their home and the impact that we have upon it. Humans are as reliant on the health of the oceans as every creature in this book is, but many of our actions are harming the fragile ecosystems these creatures need to survive.

But there is still hope. Fortunately, the ocean is immense, and its sheer size offers a way for it to recover, given time and with our help. For example, humans could begin to reverse the effects of plastic pollution if we stopped producing single-use plastics and cleaned up areas like the Great Pacific Garbage Patch. We already know that fish numbers recover dramatically in protected marine reserves, and animals will, if left undisturbed, return to and flourish in areas they were once driven out of.

As we understand better the effects that our actions have on Earth's oceans, we also learn how we can create positive change. All around the world, individuals and groups are working hard to preserve and restore the health of our waters. If each of us begins to take responsibility for our choices and encourages others to do so, then together we can ensure a future for the creatures with which we share our seas.

Ben

Index

Ben Rothery is a detail-obsessed illustrator from Norwich, via Cape Town. He combines multiple processes to create intricate and delicate illustrations and repeating patterns, full of fine detail and vibrant color.

Much of Ben's work is inspired or informed by his love of nature – he grew up wanting variously to be a shark, a dinosaur or David Attenborough crossed with Indiana Jones, but settled on illustration as a way to bring those fantasies to life on paper.

Ben works from a small studio in London, which he shares with an unnecessarily large collection of very sharp pencils.

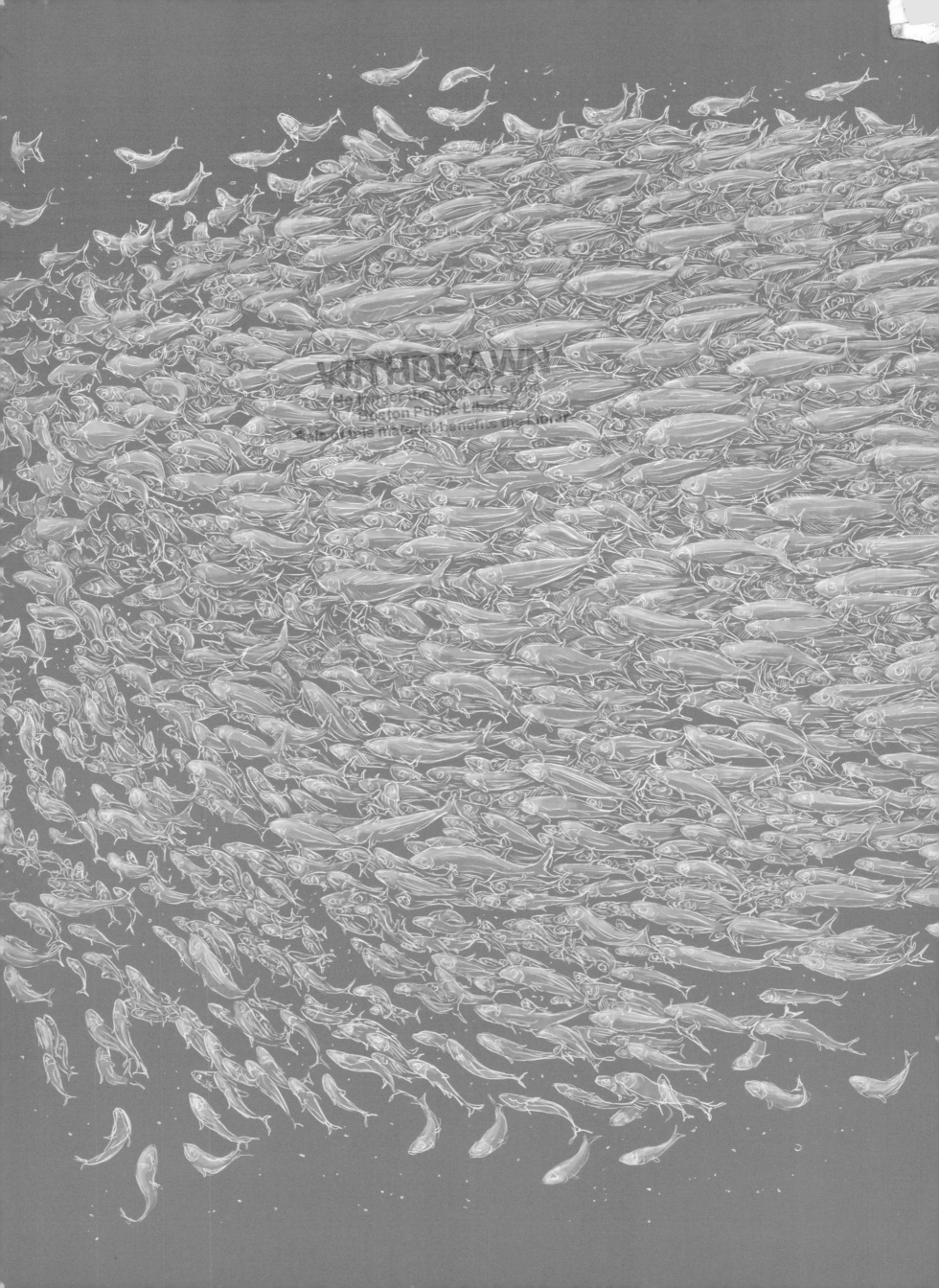